expressions

Albert Török

Albert Török

For us

CONTENTS

expressions

fire

burn fire burn
burn burn
under bridges in the night
where metal holds you
to keep the shadows far

grow fire grow
grow grow
swallow me in whole
and heat my soul
to rise above the world

go fire go
go go
take my body home
where others can't follow
but I'm not alone

rest fire rest
rest rest
settle in my heart
under the arcade
formed with my own blood

mirror

I am scared to show myself
in mirrors made by other men

what if they distort my face
kept clean in my mind?

I am aware in my well
under covering sheets of sunlight
and reflect my thoughts on you

be my mirror
and echo my soul

in the wild
among men

crowded void

your seeds
spread my chest

your roots
extend my limbs

you make me move
without my conscious contribution

your emotions nourish
your part in me

and I feel pleased
but played at the same time

I have to take my bondage off
but with each piece
I leave a memory of you behind
stranded on the roadside
decorating my past

my soul is attached
and my flesh is left
in the fragments

they turn into roadsigns
in crowded void

temples

I am here again
resting
between children of earth

and taking in light
like a beast
from labyrinth of darkness

sound enters my body
with elephant steps
in a realm
where weight is a dream

and temples grow
on path
between humans

grounded on land

summer is gone
boats on river left

I stay
with other mundanes
grounded on land

strength's trial comes
in winter-cloth
and cold enters
our body of heat

lend me your heart
I give you mine
even though unattached
we are entwined
into the same web

dust and love

samples of me
spread on sky

I am in you and in them
awake at night

Sun extends his glow
hugs Earth
and shows my body
of dust and love

I am
dust and love

I can give you only
dust and love

refuse or approve

in your present form
your silents shouts
for dust and love

the only real world

I walked my walk and talked my talk
under watching eyes of salesmen

they offered excellent life
without excellence of completion

we were converted
to chase a dream without substance

I left their row of trap
designed for lost travelers

I walk now in my sleep
dreamless
where my dreams turned to be
the only real world I know

dream up the world

hunting my hunter
in place made for hunt

eating my eater
on plate made for food

loving my lover
in universe made for love

is carved
in my heart

after all tastes join in my soul
I resign
to start my winter's rest
and dream up the world again

under your umbrella

love enters under your umbrella
in rainy days

when my gaze
shaves your hairy stuff

and superficial layers
fall in remission

your exposed soul
flickers and grows

with generations pressed
into your shopping bag of knowledge

strength

*the evening sky blushes
in your bedroom*

*when he sees the stars
under your blanket*

*sun went to sleep
with half of the world*

*behind prude mask
of twilight*

*our time comes to wake
and burn the cover of illusion on our skin*

*you light a candle with your eyes
and bend my soul with your words*

*I feel your strength
where power is measured through love*

global mind

milestones grow
on old road

people pass
in wrong direction

I turn my soul
to meet you in crowd's voice

and hold you
with no direction

you said
- I have no plans
to save us
from tomorrow -

but I save you now
without plans

while the global mind
rests on your shoulders

Albert Török

secluded part of universe

the water is so green
each of your pedals
leaves a cloud in open lagoon

and turtle from depth wonders
at your extending impressions

wrong becomes right
right turns wrong
after decades on shore

while I sit in silence
and watch waves convert to dust
in nature's training camp

the sand awakes
and becomes

foundation for skyscraper dreams
built with real stones
on this secluded part of universe

closer to your heart

I'm coming closer to your heart

with minutes
sporadically scattered in time

with present
mixing in distant past

with future
dropping its heavy shade

and showing
behind your gaze

our bond
in Earth's spell

messengers of your coming

lines tremble in ether
they are god's hair
stretched between stars

these strings are built
on their own pulse
and hold planets
on wondering paths

when you walk on them
they sound like village gongs
and are the messengers of your coming
from past or future lives

now an unknown soul
knocks on my door

would she become you
after she carves her excess on earth
and cleans herself in me?

on the throne of the land

come and take my soul
to your forest of joy

you hide your thoughts there
in the pause of creation

movement cease
in all the other places

and molecules stand
like three dimensional painting
in your living room

you go inside them
and leave sprouts of new beginnings
before reestablishing time
on the throne of the land again

engine

I was looking for perfection
while the whole assembled behind my back
and showed off to all

my shirt laughs at you
but my heart hides under horizon
and strives to mature into rising sun

wake up from sleep
we weren't born to live in a dream

we followed earth's calling
and we look at one another
with heart still broken from hard landing

let's make it whole again
it's the engine
that takes us to other stars

unintentional cruelty

*past lives in the present
and changes
with our moods or understanding
of her gifts*

*the unintentional cruelty
of raw truth
runs through us*

*future lives in the present
and changes
with our moods or understanding
of her seeds*

*the unintentional cruelty
of raw truth
runs with us*

*present lives in the present
and changes
with our moods or understanding
of her needs*

*the unintentional cruelty
of raw truth
runs in us*

Albert Török

your match

your golden age
peeks through life's wheel
and searches for interest

I widen the hole in your coat of time
to see you born and die

your moments enclosed in gold
suggest their value
to you and me

you leave a treasure chest behind
in never ending present

all the unfulfilled creatures
lurk blind
in crystal caves

they need your match
to turn the dark into sea of light

Albert Török

mix without blending

nothing
never comes close
to know
something

something
never comes close
to know
nothing

and still
both of them
meet in me

they mix without blending
then evoke the labyrinth of mind
and body

idea of life

*we are
under alien skies
where rain falls
and evaporates halfway to ground*

*power in you
guides clouds
above your wasteland
of doubts*

*let your pain
fly through the universe
on my rocket
of experience*

*and when your energy
penetrates the stars
you'll be filtered
through their idea of life*

Albert Török

loop

I swim under water

my bubbles
like ascending submarines
break the surface
and join their bigger self...

we both have the same core
we both run
to find our bigger part
in the other one

our speed became great
we passed each other
with time pressed
in fraction of moments

my glimpse
brought your fever
from your depth
to your face

you pull me
and I loop back to you
refining my trajectory
for collision

effort of experience

hanging on thread
between trust and doubt

extended
from life to death
from death to life

counting
numbers in lives
or notes in songs

and want to be certain

the effort of experience is worth
to find the answer
for the question asked

Albert Török

unaware

did you hook my heart
and let me run
at the end of thread?

you are fishing
unaware of the fisherman
angling you

the river is fast
be fit to swim
when you fall

strong current will take us
to promised land
between two shores of ideal

emotional bubbles

we ran in the park
and played under fountain's jaw

you grew rainbow around your skin
and made a water bridge

the lake caught your drops
left behind in air

they followed you everywhere

one person's band
sang his scottish-western song

a circle was closing
around around

emotional bubbles formed

they grew ready to crack
and overflow the city streets

then threaten with revolution
where lives are not lost but made

chaos and order

I feel a breeze of climate change
under my skin

my mind see demolition
in world guided by mineral anarchy

another order takes over
and we humans
relocate to abstract

my eyes see you walk on the border
of chaos and order

you hold the fabric of reality
under your sewing machine

and patch torn feelings
by remaking the past
over and over

self proclaimed limits

I am the outcome
of my meditation

I am yesterday's future
pressed into present

we both created this moment
from origins
you gave me
as gifts of your departure

dynamic days rest
on stable layers
they wrap fleeing atoms
in image power

and break
the self proclaimed limits
of boundless
intelligence

soul with two bodies

*the pure form of goddess
becomes you on my bed*

*where my seed falls
on your womb*

*and vacuum is formed
in a soul with two bodies*

chewed and digested

*over and over
in emotional impact*

*with frustration for an ideal world
where humans grow on love*

transformational chamber

where are we
in the puzzle?

you and me are collection of parts
and bond only with right ones
in a city of abundance

when our pieces match
and boundaries join
we become a mold
in god's workshop

shaping anyone
spirits or souls
who dare to come
into the transformational chamber
of earth

now

can I dissolve ignorance
with sharp looks of my mind
and pour understanding
into empty tunnels of wisdom?

loosening grasp of old customs
give a chance
to explain experience
in the light of now

meditationcrumbs@gmail.com